Home-Crafted Wines & Winemaking!

By
Gary Anderson

Copyright 2014: Gary D Anderson

ISBN-10: 150306381X

ISBN-13: 978-1503063815

Table of Contents

Introduction	Pg: 1
Why Make Your Own Wines?	Pg: 2
What You Need to Start!	Pg: 5
• The Science of Winemaking!	Pg: 7
• Yeasts & Fermentation	Pg: 7
• Oxidation & Microbes	Pg: 9
• Acidity & pH Testing	Pg: 13
• Adjusting for Acidity	Pg: 15
The Tools of Winemaking!	Pg: 17
The Essentials…	Pg: 21
A Word on Chemical Compounds…	Pg: 25
The Method…	Pg: 29
• Step 1: First Things First!	Pg: 30
• Step 2: Test & Adjust!	Pg: 31
• Step 3: Primary Fermentation!	Pg: 35
• Step 4: Secondary Fermentation!	Pg: 37
• Step 5: Settling & Stabilization!	Pg: 39
• Step 6: Final Additions & Bottling!	Pg: 41
Home Crafted Wine Recipes!	Pg: 45
• Chianti Wine	Pg: 47
• Concord Wine	Pg: 48
• Blackberry Wine	Pg: 49
• Loganberry Wine	Pg: 50
• Red Raspberry Wine	Pg: 52
• Pineapple (using fruit)	Pg: 54
• Pineapple Wine (using juice)	Pg: 56
• Peach Wine	Pg: 58
• Pear Wine	Pg: 60
• Plum Wine	Pg: 62
• Pomegranate Wine	Pg: 64
• Cherry Wine	Pg: 66
Bottling, Labeling, and Storage!	Pg: 69
Closing Comments & Resources!	Pg: 73

Introduction

Friends, food and great wine! The three just seem to go together whether it's a family dinner, summer cook-out or just about any get together where people meet and enjoy each other's company. I have found that really good wines can be made at home. If you enjoy the hands-on approach and don't mind the learning-curve of the wine making process, it can be very rewarding and fun. And yes - almost anyone willing to follow some basic guidelines can make their own great tasting wines – either traditional grape wines or wines from fruit.

One of the best wines I've had was a loganberry wine from a small vineyard near Seattle, which sold me on the idea that wonderful tasting wines could indeed be obtained, not just from grapes, but from fruits, berries and a wide variety of other natural ingredients as well.

Why make your own wines?

- The ability to use your own fruit and grapes and berries. Many people in our part of the mid-west grow pear, apple, and peach trees. Pears in particular often produce bumper crops that can be used to produce a great wine. It is also often used to blend with other fruit based wines such as elderberry or blackberry.

- Using better produce and the ability to have lower sulfite levels than commercially bottled wine. We will discuss this in more detail later but all wines require some natural compounds to provide stabilization and preservation after the fermentation and bottling.

- Experimenting with different wines, yeasts and types of blends to produce, what you consider, the perfect table wine.

- The challenge of learning the process and science of winemaking!

- Economical to make. I usually make wine in a 6 or 3 gallon batch, although single gallon batches are easy to do as well, especially if it is something new or different that you just want to try on a smaller scale until your pleased with your results. Cost including bottling will normally be less than $4.00 per gallon. When bottled that will amount to $1.50 or less per bottle.

- <u>Enjoyment of sharing something you've made with friends and family</u>. Most importantly – just a fun thing to do and something that often will include others in your family circle.

For me, wine-making seems to be a natural expression of my interests in gardening, raising grape and berry vines, and fruit trees such as pear, apple, plum and peach. I have always been intrigued with the whole concept of *"edible landscaping"*, the idea that much of the produce we use can come directly from areas "around the yard" that are also shared with flowers, shrubs and trees. Also, an interesting story was told to me by a friend who has traveled in France on several occasions. He recounted a time when he and his wife were dining at a small sidewalk café. The wine, a table wine served in a carafe, he described as simply the "very best" he had ever tasted. When they inquired if the wine could be purchased by the bottle the maître d stated that it was only available at the restaurant, it was of local origin and not bottled commercially.

In my mind, I can imagine what the perfect wine might taste like – a subtle aroma of berries or fruit, somewhat dry, with a flavorful and clean finish. What this means for me, and perhaps for you as well, is that making your own wines can be a bit of adventure as you work toward just the right blend, dryness, sweetness, acidity, alcohol levels and other factors that ultimately affect the final goal – a wine that enhances the taste of foods and is enjoyable to the palette. A wine that you might describe as "the very best" you've ever tasted!

Great Homemade Wines – Getting Started!

While home winemaking isn't that hard or difficult to do, it does require some basic knowledge and tools to succeed, plus a willingness to continue learning. It helps when your first try is successful and you bottle a great merlot – which was my experience. Later on I produced an elderberry wine that was basically "un-drinkable" – still have some bottles of that in storage. I decided to go ahead with bottling to see if it would improve with age which has not been the case. Needless to say - it's not one I share with family and friends!

The point I'm trying to make, is that you may have some failures along the way, but with the tools I am giving you in this book I believe your failings can be relatively few. In this book, I'll cover five topics that will provide the basis of *"what you need to start"*. Every successful home winemaker needs to understand the basic core concepts involved in making a great tasting wine!

- The Science – understanding the process!
- The Necessary Tools!
- Methods for small batch winemaking!
- Great Recipes!
- Bottling, Labeling & Storage!

Let's look at each of these areas individually and you should be off to a great start!

The Science of Wine...

Yeasts & Fermentation

The basic science of wine production has and continues to be centered on the effective fermentation of the natural sugars in grapes and fruit to alcohol. The alcohol in turn preserves the wine, provided the container is sealed from the outside air which would cause oxidation and spoilage.

Fermentation is a naturally occurring process as "yeast", tiny micro-organisms feed upon the sugars in grapes or fruit. There are around 1500 different species of yeasts found in nature and they are, like mushrooms, members of the "Fungi" kingdom. If you remember your Linnaeus classifications, these were basically a branch of organisms which were similar to plants but also acted, in some respects, like organisms in the "animal" kingdom as well. To settle things, the scientific world classified these organisms as a separate branch or kingdom.

Most of us are familiar with the type of yeasts used in baking bread and pizza. The types of yeasts used to produce wines are of a completely different variety. The yeast you use in winemaking has a great effect on the quality of the wine you produce. I'm sure many have experienced very disappointing results from trying to use common baking yeasts for their batch of wine. There are regions, in France for instance, where it isn't necessary to add any additional yeast for the fermentation process. There is enough natural yeast that exists in the environment and on the grapes themselves to provide for the fermentation process to continue though it's natural cycle. For most of us this is not the case, so when using local produce - either grapes, fruit, or any type of processed juice concentrate it will be necessary to add quality wine yeast – dependent on the type of wine.

These yeasts can be purchased from local stores that cater to winemaking or from online suppliers such as "Lalvin". Lalvin also provides good descriptions of their yeasts and what should be used with the type of wine you want to make. Some yeasts ferment very fast while others may continue over a longer period.

About 70% of fermentation takes place in a relatively short time, sometimes just a week or two. During the "primary" fermentation phase, the container may only be covered with a clean, dry cloth or plastic sheet, which prevents both dust and other undesirable elements from entering into the mix. During this initial process we do not need to protect the wine from oxygen, in fact oxygen is required for the yeast to do its job. Fermentation produces both alcohol and also carbon dioxide. The CO_2 blankets the top of the juice and pulp, referred to as "must" and escapes into the outside atmosphere. During the secondary stage of fermentation – the last 30% or so, an airlock device is used to "protect" the wine from oxygen while fermentation continues at a much slower rate.

Oxidation & Microbes

Cleanliness, sanitation and sterilization are practices that are extremely necessary to keep in mind during the winemaking process. Early wine makers found they could prevent spoilage by simply storing their clean, empty bottles upside down – thus preventing dust from entering the bottle prior to filling with wine. When wine is contaminated by bacteria it spoils and basically turns your wine into vinegar. I enjoy a little vinegar in salad dressing - but not by the glass. Cleaning and sterilization of glass carboys and bottles used for secondary fermentation, settling, and storage; as well as all the utensils - spoons, measuring cups, and strainers can be accomplished with hot water and a sanitizer solution. A solution of <u>*sodium-metabisulfate*</u>, which can be purchased from local stores or online is the product widely used as a sanitizer.

To clarify these practices consider the following simple definitions.

<u>Cleaning</u> – removal of apparent or visible dirt, grime or residue. This does not remove microbial bacteria.

<u>Sanitation</u> – the use of an anti-microbial agent, such as sodium-metabisulfate and hot water rinse. This will rid containers and utensils of bacterial contaminants to a large degree – but not all!

<u>Sterilization</u> – the use of heat to kill all bacterial contaminants. Hot water heated to 250 degrees Fahrenheit or above will sterilize.

Oxidization, caused by too much exposure to oxygen, can ruin the flavor of your wine turning it flat or even slightly bitter. This can occur just after "primary" fermentation if the wine is left too long without being siphoned to another container and air-locked. It is not uncommon to see winemaking kits where the primary fermenter is a 6 gallon food grade plastic bucket with a fitted lid and port for an air lock device. If you have or purchase this type of kit to get started there would be no need to utilize the cotton cloth cover we talked about earlier.

The other way wine is ruined by oxidation is by improper sealing during bottling and storage. Synthetic corks are commonly used today which allow bottles to be stored in an upright position rather than lying down. Also storage as a box type wine, using the plastic bladder inside the box, is available to home winemakers. The plastic bladder protects the wine from being exposed to air and prevents oxidation.

Temperature is vitally important to quality winemaking from the very start of the process. Proper action by the yeasts during primary fermentation as well as the other chemical changes that occur can all be hindered or even brought to a standstill by improper temperature. Temperature can also be a factor when storing wine as to high temps can literally force corks from the bottles. In general, optimum temperature for wine during the primary and secondary fermentation stages should be maintained in the range of 70-78 degrees F. Red wines will tolerate higher temperatures during fermentation, up to $84°$ F. Whites and light fruit wines do better on the lower end of the range, around $65°$ to $68°$ F. While fermentation proceeds at a faster rate in warmer temperatures, just know that if temperature gets to high – the whole batch will be ruined. Conversely, if temps get to low fermentation can come to a standstill.

Acidity & pH Testing

The pH testing of your wine needs to occur at the *beginning*, before yeast is added and the fermentation process is started. It will also be done again as the wine settles out and racked into other containers, but is absolutely necessary for fermentation to proceed correctly. It should be tested again prior to bottling, and corrected if necessary. I will talk more about these practices later within the "*Methods*" chapter, but for now we need a basic understanding of acidity, how it affects wine quality, and how it can be maintained at the proper levels.

Acidity is important in winemaking because it directly affects the taste, color and storage properties of your finished wine – either a traditional grape wine or one made from fruit or berries. If the wine is too acidic it will taste overly "tart" or "sour"; if there is not enough acidity the wine will taste "flat". In some commercially available juice concentrates the pH adjustments may have already been made - but even if you use these products it's a good idea to do your own testing as you go through the process. If you use your own fruit or grapes you will need to know these techniques regardless - it is an important skill for the home winemaker.

Acidity is measured by taking a "pH" test on your juice. The pH scale basically reads from 1 to 12 with "1" being *highly acidic* and "12" being the most *base or "non-acidic"*. Wine is best when maintained at a pH level of 3.0 to 3.5 on the scale. At this range, wine is stabilized and maintains good flavor and aroma. Acid levels are high enough to inhibit the growth of bacteria and yet low enough to avoid the characteristic "tartness" of too much acid in the taste of the wine.

A pH measurement can be obtained in a few different ways.

1. The traditional "litmus" test using the small paper strips is easy to do but difficult to obtain accurate readings in order to make adjustments.

2. A pH meter can be used, which gives a digital reading for greater accuracy. These are available from local wine making stores or online.

3. A final method, if you are really into the chemistry, is that you can test the acid content by using a "titration" method. This method doesn't show pH but rather gives you the actual amount of acid percentage that is in your solution (wine or juice). This makes it a bit easier to add the correct amount of "tartaric acid" or "Acid Blend" product to raise acidity to the desired level. It is more common in my experience, to raise

acid levels rather than lower, - also remember that when you raise acidity the pH number is getting "lower" and that 3.0 to 3.5 is our optimum target range. If you use titration readings, then the optimum <u>total acid</u> range (TA) should be at or a few points above .60% TA which equals 6 g/L.

Raising Acidity ...

This is simply a matter of adding more acid to the juice in your primary fermenter, or the glass carboy containers if the juice has progressed into the wine stage. This is accomplished by adding "Acid Blend" which is a product composed of the natural fruit acids *tartaric, citric and malic* acid.

If you have taken a "titration" reading then raising the acid level is pretty straight forward: 1 teaspoon of *Acid Blend* per gallon will increase acidity by .15% tartaric. If you prefer the use of the pH meter, as I do, you need to proceed a bit more cautiously and add the Acid Blend in small increments, perhaps only a quarter teaspoon per gallon, as you adjust PH values. Remember that the pH scale is a "*logarithmic*" scale – so an adjustment from a reading of a pH of 4.5 to 4.0 will require a different amount of added acid than would an adjustment from 4 to 3.5 – for this reason the added acids are best done by small increments. Take it carefully and then retest!

Lowering Acidity ...

As mentioned early, most adjusting will be to increase the acid content rather than lowering. If by mistake too much acid is added into the mix then this can be lowered by one of the following methods:

- <u>Prior to fermentation</u> - use a water / sugar mix of approximately 4 cups of sugar per gallon of water.
- <u>After fermentation</u> - dilute with added water or with another wine.
- <u>Chemically neutralize</u> with product such a sulfur-dioxide or similar neutralizing agent.

The Tools of Winemaking...

As with any hobby, you can start with the basics – the tools and equipment absolutely necessary for the process of making your own wines. Of course there are other tools and equipment available that can make the overall process easier, but are more costly and not entirely necessary unless you really enjoy winemaking as a hobby and intend to pursue it as long as possible. As an example of this consider the following pictures of "corkers". One is a two-lever corker that is certainly useable and comes in many winemaking kits, while the other is a floor-stand variety that holds the bottle, compresses and inserts the cork – all in one easy move. The floor model sells for approximately $135.00 but is well worth it if you have a lot to bottling to do. It provides much greater stability and leverage and makes the bottling process much easier. Some winemaking supply stores will rent them out or may even loan one to you when it's time to do your bottling!

Of course there is equipment available, such as a grape crushers, de-stemmers, wine presses and stainless steel fermentation vats that would be more necessary to a larger scale operation.

In this section I'll just cover the tools and equipment that would be needed by the home winemaker who produces 3 to 6 gallons perhaps 3 or 4 times a year.

The Essentials...

Primary Fermentation Container, some type of food grade plastic container, 5 to 6 gallons would work nicely. The container I use has a fitted lid and a port to add an airlock should I desire to use one.

Secondary Containers for fermentation and settling. For these I like 6 gallon and 3 gallon glass carboys. These glass containers allow for the necessary airlock, for less air present in the container and also for better visibility of the wine as it clarifies and settles. So far I have used the term "settling" in earlier sections and perhaps you have wondered just what is being referred to. As more and more of the sugar content in the "must" is turned into alcohol the wine's rate of fermentation slows and the yeast dies out – settling to the bottom of the containment vessel along with other fruit sediment such as seeds, grape skins or pulp. This residue is referred to as "lees" and is left behind when racking into another container by siphoning. Each additional period of settling and racking provides for a wine that is freer of sediment and cloudiness.

Airlocks, these are necessary to curtail unwanted exposure of the wine to oxygen and contamination caused by outside air.

Siphon & fitted hose, these will be used each time the wine is racked into another container and also during bottling.

Wine Thief, a long tube that allows wine to enter from the bottom and held by a small check-valve. Wine can then be used for samples and testing. Very handy item!

Bottle & Cleaning Brushes, used in cleaning everything.

Hydrometer is used to test the sugar content of juice, must, or wine. Measurement is in "Brix" percentages or "SG" (*specific gravity*).

pH Tester, I like a digital pH tester for ease of use and accuracy.

Bottle Corker, once again this item may be rentable from your local supply store.

The **chemical additives** for stabilization and sanitation – Camden Tablets, Acid Blend, sodium-metabisulfite, potassium Sorbate, and clarifying agent such as Bentonite or Issinglass.

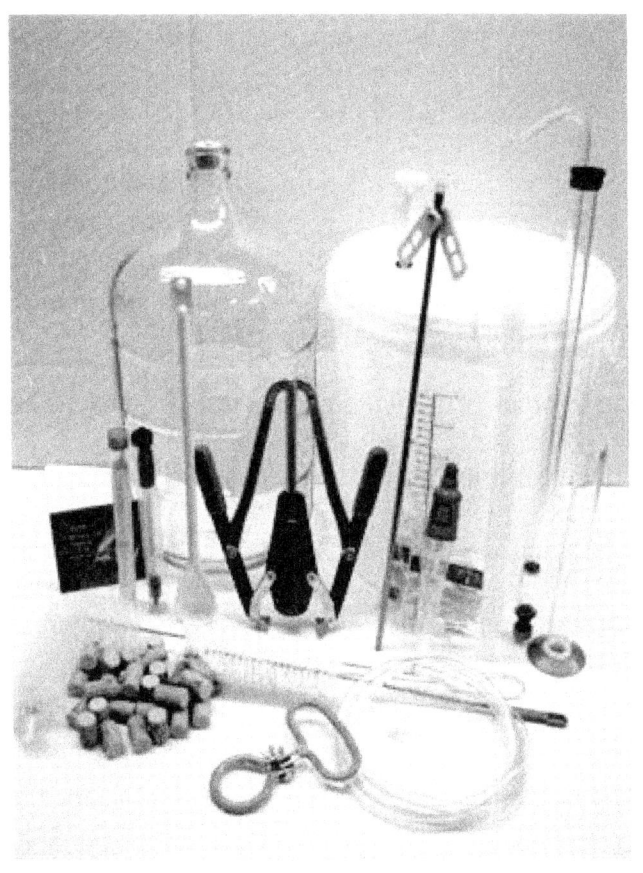

Often home winemakers will want to purchase or build their own small wine press and consider this item, which can also be used with fruit, an absolute necessity. The same might be said of the crusher/destemmer unit mentioned earlier. I guess it all depends on the amount of wine being made or the amount of fruit you have on hand to use.

It requires about 15 pounds of grapes for 1 gallon of wine. If you are not all that keen on cleaning and pressing grapes, I have found it convenient to purchase concentrated juice for use in traditional grape wines. Frozen "must" can be purchased in five-gallon containers or larger and in select vintages – so this is a viable option for those not really wanting to press your own grapes. At the end of the book I've included a separate section giving online resources for supplies, including grape juice and must. Included as well are many of the other supplies and resource materials you may need from time to time.

With fruit wines I have found that cleaning the fruit or berries, in some cases chopping them into smaller pieces (pears for instance) and then freezing - works out very well. The freezing process breaks up the cellular structure of the fruit and when thawed can easily be crushed and used.

A Word on Chemical Compounds ...

Most anyone gets a bit nervous when talking about the addition of chemical compounds to the foods we eat and drink, so we need a good understanding of just what these chemical additives are, why they are needed, and how they affect the quality of the wine we produce. Most of all – are there any detrimental effects to our health by adding these compounds to our wines?

Most of the "stabilization" compounds used in both home-crafted wines and in commercial wines are in the "sulfite" family. These are used in all commercially sold wines as a preservative to aid in long term storage. Sulfite sensitivity does affect some people, statistically about 1% of the population. To put this in perspective, the amount of sulfur compounds in most commercial wines is around 150 to 250 ppm; while dried fruit typically has around 1000 ppm. Sulfites are used in many different foods other than wine because of its antioxidant and antibacterial properties. The main difference in a wine bought at the local wine store and your home-crafted wine is that yours will contain less sulfites – usually much less! Typically, your home-crafted wines will contain less than 60 ppm of sulfites.

Other compounds such as "Acid Blend" is composed of natural "acids" found in fruits and plants. The clarifying agents or "finings" that are added to wine when it doesn't clear are compounds that draw unwanted particles to themselves and settle to the bottom of the carboy;-they are left during racking and so are not in the finished wine when bottled.

Here is a list and description of the additives common to winemaking and that are used in our recipes as well.

Sodium Metabisulfite is used widely throughout the winemaking industry. It inhibits the growth of bacteria and can also be used to sanitize bottles and equipment. It can be added directly to wine to act as a preservative when bottling. When added to wines use 1 tsp of 10% solution per gallon of wine. (For 10% solutions dissolve 4 ounces per quart of water)

Potassium Metabisulfite, like the Sodium Metabisulfite, releases sulfur dioxide when mixed with water and is used in the same way. It is approximately twice as strong as the sodium metabisulfite.

Campden Tablets are made from either sodium or potassium metabisulfite but in a precisely measured amount. The recommended amount to add to wine is one tablet per gallon of wine. Also they should be crushed and dissolved in a small amount of your wine or some water.

Yeast Nutrient aids the yeast in growing and multiplying and helps ensure that the fermentation process will continue through to completion.

Acid Blend is a mixture of citric, malic and tartaric acids and is used to increase the acidity of an acid deficient must.

Pectic Enzyme is used to break down the cellular wall structure of fruit which helps in the release and transfer of the fruit's flavor to the wine. Pectin Enzyme can also help a fruit wine to clear by removing residual pectin.

Grape Tannin is naturally found in the skins of grapes and if added can add a bit of astringency to the taste of your wine.

Oak Chips can contribute to the flavor by adding tannin and astringency. This can be added at the beginning of fermentation.

Bentonite, Isinglass or **Sparkolloid** products are used to clarify wines that are hazy or cloudy and will not clear on their own.

Potassium Sorbate is a fermentation inhibitor that is used before bottling and particularly necessary if you are sweetening your wine. It will prevent re-fermentation in the bottle.

Sugar is specified for many recipes in varying amounts. Common household sugar can be used but should not be added directly into the must. Make *sugar syrup* by dissolving sugar in water, about a 2 cup to 1 cup ratio, over a low to moderate heat on your stove. Allow to cool before adding to your wine.

The Method ...

My aim at this point is to go through the "general" areas or details of making wine. By general, I am referring to the basic "*how-to*" for whatever wine you decide to make, whether a red, white, varietal blend or fruit wine. So far we have discussed some of the basic terms, concepts, tools and equipment you need to produce your own wine – which I think is a really fun thing to do.

Hopefully you'll not feel this is "*too basic*", but if you are already familiar with the details presented in this section feel free to jump to the next where some of my favorite recipes are located. As we go through this general discussion, keep in mind that when you follow specific recipes, like the ones included in this book, that each will go into greater detail on important issues that are unique to that recipe.

Here is the general "how-to of winemaking", presented step by step!

Step 1: First-Things-First!

Clean, sanitize & sterilize is first order of business, and as has been stated, one of the most important parts of winemaking. At this point you'll need to sanitize you primary fermentation container and lid if you are using one, thermometer, hydrometer, pH tester, wine thief, funnels and any other items you will use in stirring or measuring. For a sanitizing solution you can use one ounce of sodium metabisulfate dissolved into one gallon of water. This solution can then be used as a spray or soak for your equipment and doesn't require rinsing off before using with juice or wine – just allow excess sanitizer to drain.

Prepare the fruit, grapes or produce. Note that each recipe will have somewhat differing recommendations depending on the type of fruit or berries used. But at this stage, this will usually involve crushing, mashing or smashing, chopping up and pressing-out juice from the fruit. Collect the juice and also the fruit residue for the fermentation bag. This is why proven recipes are great to have and follow.

The way *residual* fruit is used can be very recipe specific – sometimes all can go into the primary fermenter and yet with other types of fruit you may not want the seeds in your primary because they can cause bitterness or other "off" tastes in our finished wine. At times, after juice is pressed-out, the residual fruit can be placed in a mesh bag and boiled to extract additional flavor. *As a general rule* – remove all large pits, do not use a blender or food processor, and follow the recipe for preparing your specific fruit.

Step 2: Test & Adjust!

Prepare juice or "must" with the necessary additives. "*Must*" is the term used for "fermenting juice". Fill the primary fermentation container with the juice or "must" and additional water to the desired level. Some recipes call for a fermentation bag that holds the crushed fruit. This too can be placed into the primary along with the must. Once again, my primary is a 7.5 gallon food-grade plastic bucket, so I usually do a six-gallon batch. Also, given some volume loss in sediment and such, I can use either a six-gallon or 2 three-gallon glass carboys later on for secondary fermentation, clarifying and stabilizing. It's helpful during this process, if your primary has some 1 gallon graduated level marks on the outside of the container.

Test the Specific Gravity of the juice with the hydrometer. Initially, the SG of the juice needs to be in the range of 1.070 to 1.095 in sugar content. If it is near the low end of the range I would add sugar until a level of at least 1.085 is reached. Sugar is best added as syrup made by mixing two cups of sugar with one or two cups of water and heating until dissolved. Let cool and then add to the juice until the desired SG is attained. Two ounces of sugar added to one gallon of juice (or finished wine) will raise the Specific Gravity by .005 – a little math is required to adjust for three or six gallons of juice. Hydrometers sometimes have a reading for "Brix", which measures the amount of sugar in the solution, whereas SG is a measurement for the density of the juice. A Brix reading of $20°$ – $22°$ means 20% - 22 % sugar content and is the equivalent of readings 1.085 to 1.095 in SG.

Test the Acidity of the juice with your pH tester or by the "titration" method and add Acid Blend if necessary to reach a TA of approximately 3.5 pH, or a level of 6 – 7 ppt (parts per thousand) tartaric. A word of caution at this point! Note that when using the "titration" method a sample should be removed from the juice for testing and discarded afterward, the chemicals used for testing (*phenolphthalein solution* and *sodium hydroxide*) are poisonous, so care must be taken to not introduce this back into the wine. If acid content must be reduced at this early stage then dilute with water or add a base such as potassium bicarbonate.

Other additives can be introduced to the juice at this time such as "tannin" or possibly some "white oak" chips. Tannin adds "astringency" to the wine and a small amount of oak chips can add both tannins and oak barrel taste if so desired. Another important additive, if you are making a fruit based wine, is *"peptic enzyme"*. Peptic enzyme can be added at a ratio of one teaspoon per gallon of juice.

At this point crushed Campden Tablets (1 per gallon and dissolved in a small amount of water) should be added to the mix and stirred. This will kill off any "wild" yeast that may be in the must. After these adjustments and additives, cover with a lid or plastic covering and just let it rest for 24 hours.

Summary for Step 2: Test & Adjust!

- Fill Primary Fermenter with juice/water/crushed fruit to the specific level.
- Test for sugar content using the hydrometer and adjust if necessary. SG of 1.070 to 1.095
- Test for acidity and adjust if necessary. Desired pH is 3.0 to 3.5
- Introduce other additions if desired such as tannins, oak, and peptic enzyme.
- Add crushed Campden tabs, 1 per gallon.
- Cover and wait: 24 hours before adding yeast and starting the fermentation process.

Step 3: Primary Fermentation!

This is the exciting part where you see some things happening! To initiate the process of fermentation, yeast must be added to the surface of the "must". Not just any yeast, but the yeast you want for *your particular recipe.* Generally the must needs to be at least 70° F before yeast is added. It will usually be specified in the recipe itself, but you can always check the chart on the Lalvin website to see what will work or simply to experiment. Since yeast is sold as a dry packaged product it is generally a good thing to hydrate the yeast with warm water – around 90 to 100° F for a short period of time before applying to the surface of the juice. Sometimes recipes simply specify spreading the dry yeast out onto the surface of the must. In either method – don't stir the yeast into the must, just apply on the surface, cover with plastic lid or cloth, and wait. Usually within a 24 hour period you will begin to see the characteristic "foaming" which indicates that the yeast has multiplied, and is active. At this point the wine needs to be watched closely and temperature maintained within a range of approximately 68° to 78° F. Either too high or too low of a temperature can cause fermentation to stop prematurely.

The action of yeast and fermentation will form a cap across the surface of the fermenting must. This cap should periodically be broken-up or "knocked" down- but not stirred back into the must. Simply break it up twice a day or so which will allow oxygen to the surface where the microscopic yeast continues to do the job of fermentation.

After a week or so, the foaming action will slow down and begin to subside. At this point, it is time to syphon the wine into another container for "secondary" fermentation to continue. This siphoning process is referred to as *"racking"*. At this point the wine's specific gravity will probably still check greater than 1, maybe around 1.040 or a bit less. Secondary fermentation will bring it down further to our target value of 0.998 or so SG.

Summary for Step 3: Primary Fermentation!

- Add wine yeast and cover. Verify ambient temperature of 70º to 78º F.
- Watch for foaming action within 24 hours or so.
- Twice daily, punch down cap that is present on top surface of must. Do not stir!
- Continue approximately one week, say 5 to 8 days until fermentation noticeably slows and check of SG reading of 1.040 or lower.

Step 4: Secondary Fermentation – First racking!

Racking into your secondary fermentation container, at this stage a glass carboy, is an easy process if you are able to station your new container lower than your primary. Take care when moving the primary fermentation bucket not to jostle or mix up sediment back into the wine. It is at this point much of the sediment or "lees" can be left behind and discarded. The type of siphon tube I use draws the wine up into a larger, hard plastic tube and then allows it to transfer by another *flexible* tube, into the new container. One thing you need to be watchful about is in not allowing the siphon tube to drop into the sediment at the bottom of your primary - pulling sediment into your new container. If this does happen it isn't any real cause for concern but will just have to "settle out" again. In all likelihood you will rack your wine several times during the whole process as the wine continues to slowly ferment, stabilize and settle. Only when this process is finished can the new wine be bottled.

Summary for Step 4: Secondary Fermentation – First Racking!

- If a fermentation bag (pulp fermentation) has been used during primary fermentation, remove it from the must squeezing out juice from the bag back into the primary. Discard contents of the bag.
- Remember to use tools and equipment that have been sanitized!
- Rack the wine into the new container, the glass carboy which will be used for secondary fermentation. Leave as much of the sediment or "lees" <u>behind</u> as possible.
- Top off wine with additional water and apply the airlock for the container.
- Wait; allow two to four weeks before racking again. This will vary per different types of wine.
- Check from time to time to ensure integrity of your airlock.

Step 5: Settling & Stabilization!

This step progresses with additional settling and racking. As fermentation continues at a much slower rate, more of the yeast dies and settles to the bottom of the carboy as precipitate residue. Each time you rack into another clean carboy you leave this old sediment behind and your wine should become clearer. Stability is reached at the point where you are only seeing an occasional CO^2 bubble rise to the surface. As you check the specific gravity with your hydrometer, you will notice lower readings which indicate that sugar content is getting progressively lower and alcohol content higher. Some wines will finish and stabilize around the 0.998 mark while other sweeter wines, such as a white zinfandel may reach 1.010 and go no lower.

It doesn't hurt to simply allow the wine to bulk age in this manner as long as you maintain a good airlock on the carboy – just remember to "top off" the wine each time you rack as you will lose some liquid with the sediment you leave in the bottom of the carboy. Stabilization is important to achieve before bottling, so there is no need to try to rush this along. A friend of mine who bottled too soon experienced a rude awakening one evening as corks exploded out of his stored bottles of blackberry wine. In his excited anticipation, he had simply bottled his wine before it had completely finished fermentation. Just remember that there is no rush to bottle at this point – the wine will improve with every period of bulk-aging and racking.

In general, your home-crafted wine will be racked the first time (after primary fermentation) after a week or so, again in four weeks – after secondary fermentation, and then every two to three months until clear and sediment becomes minimal.

Summary for Step 5: Settling & Stabilization!

- Remember to use tools and equipment that have been sanitized!
- Rack again after secondary fermentation, leaving sediment, test for SG and taste!
- Top off wine with additional water and apply the airlock for the container.
- Do again after two to three months, and again, and yet again until wine is clear and stable.

Step 6: Final Additions & Bottling!

When your wine is stable it is *almost* ready to be bottled. There are several additives to consider before proceeding, some of these are optional and some are not.

If a wine is a bit hazy or cloudy after several racks, a *clarifying agent* can be added such as Bentonite, Isinglass or Sparkolloid. Simply follow the directions for the amount of wine you have. This process will involve another waiting period where precipitate is allowed to settle out of the wine before bottling.

The addition of Campden tabs – approximately ½ to 1 tab per gallon will help preserve both the color and flavor of the wine for longer term storage. This is more necessary for white & fruit wines and somewhat less so for red wines.

The addition of a "*fermentation inhibitor*" such as Potassium Sorbate is necessary if you wish to sweeten your wine before bottling. Add ½ teaspoon per gallon *before* adding sugar syrup to your finished wine.

If you desire a sweeter wine then this is the time to add the sugar/water mix. Check SG as you add in small increments and remember that 2 ounces of sugar per gallon will raise the specific gravity reading by ".005". Anything with a SG of 1 or greater is what I would consider a "sweet" wine so this is your opportunity to make it "just the way you like"! If you have used the inhibitor and sweetened your wine it is also a good idea to wait another month before bottling as stabilizers will sometimes cause additional sedimentation.

Siphon your wine into clean, sanitized bottles and seal with a good quality cork. Synthetic corks are popular because wine bottles can be stored in an upright position rather than lying on their side. Make sure corks are sanitized as well, by allowing them to soak for 30 minutes or so in a sanitizing solution of sodium metabisulfite. Fill bottles to about a "two finger width" level from the bottom of the cork, - this will usually allow enough room for the air inside the bottle to compress without forcing the cork back up and out of the bottle. If you are using traditional cork rather than the synthetic variety leave your bottles upright for a few days before laying them on their sides. Synthetic corked bottles, as already mentioned, can be stored upright. Finally, be sure to label and date your wine!

Summary for Step 6: Final Additions & Bottling!

- Optional - Add clarifying agent / stir vigorously / top off and airlock / allow 10 to 14 days for settling before bottling.
- Add Campden tabs: ½ to 1 tab per gallon. This helps prevent oxidation and acts to preserve both color and taste.
- Add Potassium Sorbate: ½ tsp / gallon if you plan on "sweetening" your wine.
- Add sugar solution to desired taste. Add in small increments and re-test with hydrometer.
- If sweetened – airlock and allow to settle for another month.
- Sanitize bottles and corks with solution of sodium-metabisulfite.
- Siphon wine into bottles, cork and label. Remember "2-finger width" rule when filling – do not overfill bottles!
- Store upright for at least two days and then lay bottle on side unless synthetic corks are used.

Recipes for Great Home-Crafted Wines!

In this section I've included a dozen different wines that I enjoy and that I feel have wide spread appeal; - remember there are many more awaiting *your* discovery. Now that you are more familiar with basic wine-making methods, you may even decide to develop some recipes of your own! To me the best hobbies are those where you continue to grow in your knowledge and skill level – winemaking certainly fits that description.

As you try the following recipes you'll generally discover things that you want to do differently next time, you will also make a few mistakes and enjoy some successes. For these reasons alone, it's a good idea to keep a notebook handy for your thoughts and ideas, dates you do racking, temperatures, acid and sugar readings, and a host of other details you may want to remember. This will become important as you make slight adjustments to batches of different wines and also for details of things you may want to change the next time you make a particular wine.

These recipes are all for <u>one gallon</u> batches. If you want to go with larger amounts, as I often do, just increase your ingredients accordingly. I have, at various times, used one gallon bottles for secondary fermentation and finishing out the wine, but prefer to use either six or three gallon carboys. Airlocks and stoppers for these different sized bottles are available at your local wine-making supply store or through online resources.

As you use these recipes, and the many others you will discover along your journey, keep in mind that "*home-crafted*" wines are those produced by using your own unique tastes and ideas. While you might initially follow recipes closely, in due time you'll be adding your own special touches to your wines, - that's the whole idea of a *home-crafted* wine. It may be a blend of "reds" for the perfect red table wine, or a blending of fruit wines such as pear and blackberry in a ratio that you feel is unique and tasteful. There may be other instances where different fruits can be blended and go through fermentation together for a unique flavor and aroma combination. You get the idea! Home-crafted wines should ultimately reflect your personal tastes and skills.

Chianti

32 ounces of Red Grape Concentrate

½ gallon warm water

Sugar syrup (one part water to two parts sugar dissolved) to reach Specific Gravity of 1.095

Test for pH and add *Acid Blend* if necessary to reach a pH of 3.5

1 Campden Tablet, crushed

1 teaspoon of *Yeast Nutrient*

½ ounce of oak chips

Wine Yeast, Lalvin RC-212 (one packet for 1gallon or 5 gallon batch)

***

Steps 1 & 2: Except do not add oak chips until *later* racking when SG of 1.010 is reached.

Step 3: Ferment for 5 days until SG of 1.040 is reached then continue into step 4, secondary fermentation.

Step 4: Rack into glass container leaving lees and sediment in primary, top off with sugar/water mix and airlock. Allow 3 weeks in secondary then rack again.

Step 5 & 6: Rack every two months until wine is clear, stable, and has no sediment. At this time follow step 6 for sweetening (if desired) and bottling.

Note: Rack every two months until wine is clear, stable, and has no sediment. At this time follow step 6 for sweetening (if desired) and bottling. Age twelve months or more.

Concord Wine

32 ounces Frozen Grape Concentrate

¾ gallon warm water

Sugar syrup (one part water to two parts sugar dissolved) to reach Specific Gravity of 1.095

Test for pH and add *Acid Blend* if necessary to reach a pH of 3.5

1 Campden Tablet, crushed

½ tsp of Pectic Enzyme

1 teaspoon of *Yeast Nutrient*

Wine Yeast, Lalvin RC-212 (one packet for 1gallon or 5 gallon batch)

***

Steps 1 & 2: Mix all ingredients except yeast into primary, cover and allow to set 24 hours.

Step 3: Add wine yeast and ferment for 6 to 7 days until SG of 1.040 is reached then continue into step 4, secondary fermentation.

Step 4: Rack into glass container leaving lees and sediment in primary, top off with sugar/water mix and airlock. Allow 3 weeks in secondary then rack again.

Step 5 & 6: Rack every two months until wine is clear, stable, and has no sediment. At this time follow step 6 for sweetening (if desired) and bottling.

Note: Age 3 to 6 months or more.

Blackberry Wine

5 pounds of Blackberries (fresh or frozen)

Water (enough to make up one gallon)

Sugar syrup (one part water to two parts sugar dissolved) to reach Specific Gravity of 1.095

Test for pH and add *Acid Blend* if necessary to reach a pH of 3.5

1 Campden Tablet, crushed

½ tsp of Pectic Enzyme

1 teaspoon of *Yeast Nutrient*

Wine Yeast, Lalvin 71B-1122 suggested (one packet for 1gallon or 5 gallon batch)

***

Steps 1 & 2: If using frozen berries allow them to thaw. Lightly crush fruit and put it into the fermentation bag. Mix juice, fermentation bag (crushed fruit), and all other ingredients (except yeast) into primary, cover and allow to set 24 hours.

Step 3: Add wine yeast and ferment for 6 to 7 days until SG of 1.040 is reached then continue into step 4, secondary fermentation.

Step 4: Remove fermentation bag and lightly press out residual liquid back into primary. Rack into glass container leaving lees and sediment in primary, top off with wine or sugar/water mix and airlock. Allow 2 weeks in secondary then rack again.

Step 5 & 6: Rack every two months until wine is clear, stable, and has no sediment. At this time follow step 6 for sweetening (if desired) and bottling. Age 6 months or more.

Loganberry Wine

5 pounds of Loganberries (fresh or frozen)

Water (enough to make up one gallon)

Sugar syrup (one part water to two parts sugar dissolved) to reach Specific Gravity of 1.095

Test for pH and add *Acid Blend* if necessary to reach a pH of 3.5

1 Campden Tablet, crushed

½ tsp of Pectic Enzyme

1 teaspoon of *Yeast Nutrient*

Wine Yeast, Lalvin 71B-1122 suggested (one packet for 1 gallon or 5 gallon batch)

***

Steps 1 & 2: If using frozen berries allow them to thaw. Lightly crush fruit and put it into the fermentation bag. Mix juice, fermentation bag (crushed fruit), and all other ingredients (except yeast) into primary, cover and allow to set 24 hours.

Step 3: Add wine yeast and ferment for 6 to 7 days until SG of 1.040 is reached then continue into step 4, secondary fermentation.

Step 4: Remove fermentation bag and lightly press out residual liquid back into primary. Rack into glass container leaving lees and sediment in primary, top off with wine or sugar/water mix and airlock. Allow 2 weeks in secondary then rack again.

Step 5 & 6: Rack every two months until wine is clear, stable, and has no sediment. At this time follow step 6 for sweetening (if desired) and bottling.

Note: Age 6 months or more.

Red Raspberry Wine

4 to 5 pounds of Red Raspberries (fresh or frozen)

Water (enough to make up one gallon)

Sugar syrup (one part water to two parts sugar dissolved) to reach Specific Gravity of 1.095

Test for pH and add *Acid Blend* if necessary to reach a pH of 3.5

1 Campden Tablet, crushed

½ tsp of Pectic Enzyme

1 teaspoon of *Yeast Nutrient*

Wine Yeast, Lalvin 71B-1122 suggested (one packet for 1gallon or 5 gallon batch)

***

Steps 1 & 2: If using frozen berries allow them to thaw. Lightly crush fruit and put it into the fermentation bag. Mix juice, fermentation bag (crushed fruit), and all other ingredients (except yeast) into primary, cover and allow to set 24 hours.

Step 3: Add wine yeast and ferment for 6 to 7 days until SG of 1.040 is reached then continue into step 4, secondary fermentation.

Step 4: Remove fermentation bag and lightly press out residual liquid back into primary. Rack into glass container leaving lees and sediment

in primary, top off with wine or sugar/water mix and airlock. Allow 2 weeks in secondary then rack again.

Step 5 & 6: Rack every two months until wine is clear, stable, and has no sediment. At this time follow step 6 for sweetening (if desired) and bottling.

Note: Age 6 months or more.

Pineapple Wine (from fruit)

3 to 4 pounds of Pineapple, (having removed rind & core, chop ripe fruit into small pieces)

Water (enough to make up one gallon)

Sugar syrup (one part water to two parts sugar dissolved) to reach Specific Gravity of 1.090

Test for pH and add *Acid Blend* if necessary to reach a pH of 3.5

1 Campden Tablet, crushed

½ tsp of Pectic Enzyme

1 teaspoon of *Yeast Nutrient*

Wine Yeast, Lalvin 71B-1122 suggested (one packet for 1gallon or 5 gallon batch)

***

Steps 1 & 2: Put chopped fruit into fermentation bag then crush fruit and press juice into the primary fermenter. Mix juice, fermentation bag (crushed fruit), and all other ingredients (except yeast) into primary, cover and allow to set 24 hours.

Step 3: Add wine yeast and ferment for 6 to 7 days until SG of 1.040 is reached then continue into step 4, secondary fermentation.

Step 4: Remove fermentation bag and lightly press out residual liquid back into primary. Rack into glass container leaving lees and sediment

in primary, top off with sugar/water mix and airlock. Allow 3 weeks in secondary then rack again.

Step 5 & 6: Rack every two months until wine is clear, stable, and has no sediment. At this time follow step 6 for sweetening (if desired) and bottling.

Note: Age 3 to 6 months or more.

Pineapple Wine (from juice)

1.5 quarts (48 oz.) of Pineapple Juice, (no preservatives added)

Water (enough to make up one gallon)

Sugar syrup (one part water to two parts sugar dissolved) to reach Specific Gravity of 1.090

Test for pH and add *Acid Blend* if necessary to reach a pH of 3.5

1 Campden Tablet, crushed

½ tsp of Pectic Enzyme

1 teaspoon of *Yeast Nutrient*

Champagne Yeast, Lalvin EC-1118 suggested (one packet for 1gallon or 5 gallon batch)

***

Steps 1 & 2: Mix all ingredients except yeast into primary, cover and allow to set 24 hours.

Step 3: Add wine yeast and ferment for 6 to 7 days until SG of 1.040 is reached - then continue into step 4, secondary fermentation.

Step 4: Rack into glass container leaving lees and sediment in primary, top off with sugar/water mix and airlock. Allow 3 weeks in secondary then rack again.

Step 5 & 6: Rack every two months until wine is clear, stable, and has no sediment. At this time follow step 6 for sweetening (if desired) and bottling.

Note: Age 3 to 6 months or more.

Peach Wine

5 to 6 pounds of Peaches, (having removed pits, cut into smaller pieces)

Water (enough to make up one gallon)

Sugar syrup (one part water to two parts sugar dissolved) to reach Specific Gravity of 1.085

Test for pH and add *Acid Blend* if necessary to reach a pH of 3.5

1 Campden Tablet, crushed

½ tsp of Pectic Enzyme

¼ tsp of Tannin powder

1 teaspoon of *Yeast Nutrient*

Wine Yeast, Lalvin 71B-1122 suggested (one packet for 1gallon or 5 gallon batch)

***

Steps 1 & 2: Put chopped fruit into fermentation bag then crush fruit and press juice into the primary fermenter. Mix juice, fermentation bag (crushed fruit), and all other ingredients (except yeast) into primary, cover and allow to set 24 hours.

Step 3: Add wine yeast and ferment for 6 to 7 days until SG of 1.040 is reached then continue into step 4, secondary fermentation.

Step 4: Remove fermentation bag and lightly press out residual liquid back into primary. Rack into glass container leaving lees and sediment

in primary, top off with sugar/water mix and airlock. Allow 1 week in secondary then rack again.

Step 5 & 6: Rack every two months until wine is clear, stable, and has no sediment. At this time follow step 6 for sweetening (if desired) and bottling.

Note: Age 6 months or more.

Pear Wine

8 pounds of Pears, (having removed core & stem, cut into smaller pieces)

1 cup of white grape concentrate or additional 32 oz. pear juice (no preservatives)

Water (enough to make up one gallon)

Sugar syrup (one part water to two parts sugar dissolved) to reach Specific Gravity of 1.085

Test for pH and add *Acid Blend* if necessary to reach a pH of 3.5

1 Campden Tablet, crushed

½ tsp of Pectic Enzyme

1 teaspoon of *Yeast Nutrient*

Wine Yeast, Lalvin 71B-1122 suggested (one packet for 1gallon or 5 gallon batch)

***

Steps 1 & 2: Put chopped fruit directly into the primary fermenter. Mix juice, crushed fruit, and all other ingredients (except yeast) into primary, cover and allow to set 24 hours.

Step 3: Add wine yeast and ferment for 6 to 7 days until SG of 1.040 is reached then continue into step 4, secondary fermentation.

Step 4: Rack into glass container leaving lees and sediment in primary, top off with sugar/water mix and airlock. Allow 1 week in secondary then rack again.

Step 5 & 6: Rack every two months until wine is clear, stable, and has no sediment. At this time follow step 6 for sweetening (if desired) and bottling.

Note: Age 6 months or more.

Plum Wine

5 to 6 pounds of Plums, (having removed pits, cut into smaller pieces)

Water (enough to make up one gallon)

Sugar syrup (one part water to two parts sugar dissolved) to reach Specific Gravity of 1.085

Test for pH and add *Acid Blend* if necessary to reach a pH of 3.5

1 Campden Tablet, crushed

½ tsp of Pectic Enzyme

1 teaspoon of *Yeast Nutrient*

Wine Yeast, Lalvin 71B-1122 suggested (one packet for 1 gallon or 5 gallon batch)

***

Steps 1 & 2: Put chopped fruit into fermentation bag then crush fruit and press juice into the primary fermenter. Mix juice, fermentation bag (crushed fruit), and all other ingredients (except yeast) into primary, cover and allow to set 24 hours.

Step 3: Add wine yeast and ferment for 6 to 7 days until SG of 1.040 is reached then continue into step 4, secondary fermentation.

Step 4: Remove fermentation bag and lightly press out residual liquid back into primary. Rack into glass container leaving lees and sediment

in primary, top off with sugar/water mix and airlock. Allow 1 week in secondary then rack again.

Step 5 & 6: Rack every two months until wine is clear, stable, and has no sediment. At this time follow step 6 for sweetening (if desired) and bottling.

Note: Age 6 months or more.

Pomegranate Wine

6 or 7 Pomegranates, (having removed pits, cut into smaller pieces)

1 pint white grape juice

Water (enough to make up one gallon)

Sugar syrup (one part water to two parts sugar dissolved) to reach Specific Gravity of 1.085

Test for pH and add *Acid Blend* if necessary to reach a pH of 3.5

1 Campden Tablet, crushed

½ tsp of Pectic Enzyme

1 teaspoon of *Yeast Nutrient*

Champagne Yeast, Lalvin EC-1118 suggested (one packet for 1gallon or 5 gallon batch)

***

Steps 1 & 2: Wash and peel ripened fruit and remove the seeds. Chop seeds and put into the fermentation bag. Crush fruit (seeds) and squeeze as much juice into the primary fermenter as you can. Mix juice, fermentation bag (crushed fruit), and all other ingredients (except yeast) into the primary, cover and allow to set 24 hours.

Step 3: Add wine yeast and ferment for 6 to 7 days until SG of 1.040 is reached then continue into step 4, secondary fermentation.

Step 4: Remove fermentation bag and lightly press out residual liquid back into primary. Rack into glass container leaving lees and sediment in primary, top off with sugar/water mix and airlock. Allow 3 weeks in secondary then rack again.

Step 5 & 6: Rack every two months until wine is clear, stable, and has no sediment. At this time follow step 6 for sweetening (if desired) and bottling.

Note: Age 6 months.

Cherry Wine

5 pounds of Cherries, either sweet or sour variety, (remove pits, cut into smaller pieces)

Water (enough to make up one gallon)

Sugar syrup (one part water to two parts sugar dissolved) to reach Specific Gravity of 1.085

Test for pH and add *Acid Blend* if necessary to reach a pH of 3.5

1 Campden Tablet, crushed

½ tsp of Pectic Enzyme

1 teaspoon of *Yeast Nutrient*

Wine Yeast, Lalvin 71B-1122 suggested (one packet for 1gallon or 5 gallon batch)

***

Steps 1 & 2: Put chopped fruit into fermentation bag then crush fruit and press juice into the primary fermenter. Mix juice, fermentation bag (crushed fruit), and all other ingredients (except yeast) into primary, cover and allow to set 24 hours.

Step 3: Add wine yeast and ferment for 6 to 7 days until SG of 1.040 is reached then continue into step 4, secondary fermentation.

Step 4: Remove fermentation bag and lightly press out residual liquid back into primary. Rack into glass container leaving lees and sediment

in primary, top off with sugar/water mix and airlock. Allow 1 week in secondary then rack again.

Step 5 & 6: Rack every two months until wine is clear, stable, and has no sediment. At this time follow step 6 for sweetening (if desired) and bottling.

Note: Age 6 months.

Bottling, Labeling & Storage...

Some of the practical details of bottling have already been covered as Step 6 in the "Methods" section, but I'll take some time here to reiterate important aspects of bottling and storage and also share in the following section some great resources for home-crafted wines and winemaking!

Here again is a brief summary of the things to know and do when it's time to bottle your wine.

Summary for Step 6: Final Additions & Bottling!

- Optional - Add clarifying agent / stir vigorously / top off and airlock / allow 10 to 14 days for settling *before* bottling.
- Add Campden tabs: ½ to 1 tab per gallon. This helps prevent oxidation and acts to preserve both color and taste.
- Add Potassium Sorbate: ½ tsp / gallon if you plan on "sweetening" your wine.
- Add sugar solution to desired taste. Add in small increments and re-test with hydrometer.
- If sweetened – airlock and allow to settle for another month.
- Sanitize bottles and corks with solution of sodium-metabisulfite.

- Siphon wine into bottles, cork and label. Remember "2-finger width" rule when filling – do not overfill bottles!
- Store upright for at least two days and then lay bottle on side unless synthetic corks are used.

Bottles can be purchased in the standard 750 ml size and in clear, green, or blue glass. Also the 375 ml and 1.5 L magnum sizes are available from local winemaking supply stores. Corks, labels, and heat-shrinkable caps are also available and really give your bottled wine a very stylish look for gift giving or display.

Once bottled, it is time to store your wine for the recommended aging period outlined by each recipe. Remember this is only a recommendation – I think part of the *"learning curve"* in winemaking is to *taste test* your wines on the day you bottle and periodically until the full recommended aging period is reached.

The *ideal* storage conditions for your bottles of wine may be difficult to achieve, maybe even impossible unless you have the perfect wine cellar. They are as follows:

- An ambient temperature of 55°F with only about a 1° to 3° daily temperature variation.
- A relative humidity of 70%
- Darkness with little or no vibration.

Once again, an ideal storage environment might be difficult to achieve, but is yet a definite goal to aim toward. It you store, as I did, with bottles boxed, in an extra closet or basement, at an ambient temp of 74°F, it should not ruin your wine – provided it was stable when bottled!

Closing Comments & Resources...

Should you *not* have a store for winemaking supplies in your community, there are a great many online resources from which to choose. These suppliers, aside from the necessary equipment, additive and bottling supplies, can also provide *juice bases and purees* for many varieties of grapes, fruits and berries. After all, you may have a bumper crop of pears - but no locally grown loganberries or cherries, so for variety you can purchase some of your winemaking ingredients from other locations and sources.

One such supplier is "Vintner's Harvest" which supplies both fruit bases and purees to winemakers through its distributors. I will list some of these in this section but you can go directly to the "Vintner's Harvest" website to find distributors near you.

One of the differences in a *"fruit base"* and a *"puree"* is that the fruit base contains the crushed fruit and juice, while a "puree" is basically the same product in a more processed state. Often the puree is a smoother consistency, tends to be more concentrated and often has seeds removed. Either product would be measured in pound-for-pound fashion as called for in different recipes, although with a puree you could use approximately 10% less than the recommended recipe amount. Another important detail is that most *fruit bases* require the use of a fermentation or strainer bag in the primary fermentation vessel, while a *puree* can conveniently be put directly into the must.

Here are some online resources that can help you along with all the ingredients necessary for great home winemaking!

- Midwest Supplies: www.midwestsupplies.com
- Craft Winemaking: www.craftwinemaking.com
- Vintner's Harvest: www.vintnersharvest.com
- The Wine & Hop Shop: www.wineandhop.com
- High Gravity: www.highgravity.com
- Bottle Your Brand: www.bottleyourbrand.com
- Brehm Vineyards: www.brehmvineyards.com

At this point, you have all the tools and knowledge needed to succeed in making your own home-crafted wines. As you can see, it doesn't require an extensive background in winemaking, simply a willingness to learn and the ability to follow basic techniques and practices. I encourage you to keep a wine journal for each batch of wine you produce. Make careful notes on sugar and acid measurements, temperatures, the additives you use, and also the personal insights you gain, as you progress through each step.

I've written this book, not only to share some outstanding recipes for different wines, but to bring together the basic aspects of winemaking in clear and logical steps. These steps apply- regardless of the types of fruit, grapes or produce you choose to use. Of course there are many, many other things to learn, which is why there are college-level studies devoted to viniculture and winemaking. In other words, the whole aspect of winemaking is wide open for those interested enough to pursue the skills and knowledge. While I'm not involved in commercial winemaking or vineyards, it is still interesting to learn new things that might make a procedure easier and more efficient, or that helps produce a better quality wine.

My hope is that I have provided a good foundation to start, succeed, and to really enjoy your journey into the world of winemaking!

Thank you for taking time to purchase and read "*Home-Crafted Wines & Winemaking*". If you would like to contact me with question or comments you can do so at the following email address:

Email: ganderson61@cox.net

Your comments and reviews are much appreciated!

CPSIA information can be obtained
at www.ICGtesting.com
Printed in the USA
LVOW13s1556060218
565495LV00011B/387/P